**ROGERS MEMORIAL
LIBRARY**

D1397350

Baby Booties

Eighteen pretty pairs to knit

Caroline de Hugo

Knitting instructions by Élisabeth Tzinakas

Photography by Richard Boutin
Styling by Vania Leroy

Illustrations by Anne Sohier-Fournel

Contents

ROGERS MEMORIAL
LIBRARY

Yarns

When it comes to shopping for yarns — both in stores and on the internet — you'll be spoilt for choice. For a baby, it's better to choose yarns that are soft to the touch and that won't irritate the delicate skin of his or her little feet. Choose natural materials, such as pure wool, alpaca, cashmere, cotton, linen or silk, which are much more environmentally friendly than synthetic materials. If your baby suffers from eczema, always make the booties in cotton. Babies are delicate creatures, so it's better to protect them from harmful chemicals for as long as possible.

It is a good idea to choose a yarn that is not too thick. Thinner yarns enable you to create finer, more refined work. You will find the recommended needle size on the label of the ball of yarn. Choose yarn that can be knitted with 2.75 mm (US 2/UK 12), 3 mm (US 2/UK 11) or even 3.5 mm (US 4/UK 10) needles. If you aren't used to knitting with thin yarn, you'll need need to take a little more care, but remember that booties are small, quickly made pieces that will never take you more than one or two evenings to make.

For washing, choose 'green' laundry detergents. They clean just as well as chemical laundry detergents. Or, as my mother did and as I did for my children, take the five minutes needed to wash items by hand, using Marseille or Castille soap. That way, you'll extend the life of the most delicate booties, and your baby will smell lovely!

Important notes: Please make sure that any buttons or accessories used — such as beads, sequins, bells, fabric flowers or ribbons — are attached securely so that your baby cannot pull them off and put them in their mouth. It is very important to check that they are still tightly fastened after each and every wash.

Avoid 'hairy' yarns such as angora or mohair, because such fibres carry a risk of choking. Young infants become fascinated by their feet very early on and can easily pull off a few angora fibres to put in their mouth.

Equipment

You hardly need anything to knit: a pair of needles and a ball of wool will do. But for the purists, here is a brief survey of the equipment you may need to make the patterns in this book.

Standard needles

These are available in wood, metal or plastic. They are pointed at one end and have a head at the other end to hold the stitches on. A number indicating the needle size — 1.5 mm to 10 mm ($\frac{1}{16}$ inch to ½ inch) in diameter — is often engraved on the head.

Double-pointed needles

These are generally made of metal and sold in sets of four or five. You can use them to put stitches on hold or else to make a cable stitch more easily.

Needle size conversion chart

Metric (mm)	US	UK/Canada
2	0	14
2.25	1	13
2.75	2	12
3	–	11
3.25	3	10
3.5	4	–
3.75	5	9
4	6	8
4.5	7	7
5	8	6
5.5	9	5
6	10	4
6.5	10½	3
7	–	2
7.5	–	1
8	11	0
9	13	00
10	15	000
12	17	–
15–16	19	–
19	35	–
25	50	–

Wool needle

This is a sewing needle with a rounded point and a wide eye that you use to sew the different sections of a knitted piece together without running the risk of pricking yourself.

Box of pins

A few pins will help to hold together the different sections of your knitted piece while you sew them up.

Scissors

A small pair of pointed scissors is essential for any self-respecting knitter.

Tape measure

There are very practical retractable models available, which take up very little space. Failing that, you can of course use a good ruler.

Row-counter

This little counter is threaded onto one of the needles, or attached to the knitting. You just need to give it a flick with your finger tip at the end of each row. It will spare you many mistakes.

Other equipment

Related equipment includes a pompom circle, a steam iron and an ironing cloth. What you need will depend on the project.

Techniques and stitches

Often, knitting instructions look like a secret code: completely incomprehensible. In this book, so as not to put off beginner knitters by overloading the text with abbreviations, I chose to write out the instructions in full. Hopefully you will find it easier to follow.

I - Starting and finishing

Casting on stitches

Make a slip knot:

1. Take the end of the yarn from the ball in your left hand, and allow a short length of yarn to hang down, which will be used later for finishing and sewing up. Slip the yarn under the fingers of this hand and wrap it clockwise around the forefinger and middle finger. Loop the yarn round a second time, closer to the base of the two fingers.

2. Holding the two yarn ends taut between your thumb and ring finger, take a knitting needle in your right hand and slip it under the first loop (A).

3. Catch the second loop from behind with the point of the needle and pull it through the first, towards the tip of the fingers.

4. Slip the two fingers out of the loop and pull gently on the two ends of the yarn to tighten the knot around the needle (B).

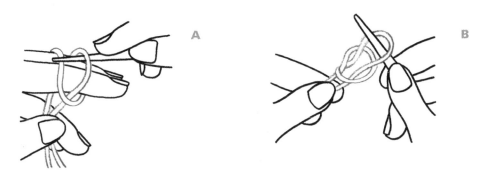

... then continue the beginning row

1. Pass the needle with the slip knot to your left hand. Take the second needle in your right hand and insert it, left to right, into the slip knot (A).

2. Take the yarn from the ball in your right hand and loop it, anti-clockwise, around the right needle, behind the left needle (B).

3. Gently pull the right needle through the first loop to bring a second loop to the front (C).

4. Insert the tip of the left needle into the new loop to pass the stitch to that needle (D).

5. Repeat this process as many times as needed to make the required number of stitches (E).

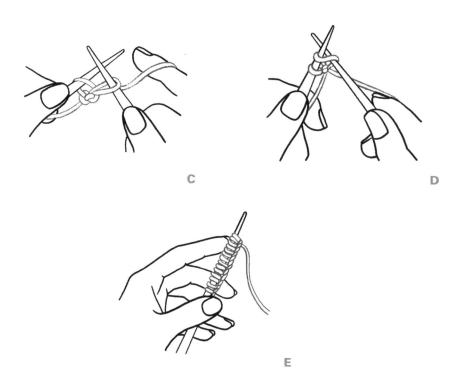

C

D

E

Casting off stitches

To finish a piece of knitting, the stitches need to be cast off so that they don't unravel. To do this, you just need to work 2 stitches (A), then slip the first one over the second (B).

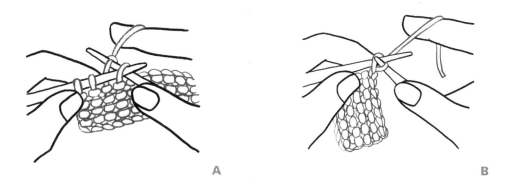

A

B

Garter stitch and knit stitches

Every row is worked in knit. Follow the steps below to make a knit stitch.

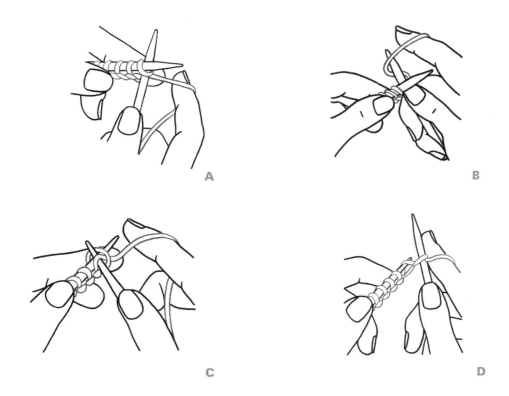

A   B

C   D

Stocking stitch and purl stitches

Odd rows are worked in knit, even rows in purl. (For reverse stocking stitch, simply work odd rows in purl and even rows in knit.) Follow the steps below to make a purl stitch.

A   B   C

Single rib (1x1)

This is worked over 2 rows and an even number of stitches.
Row 1: Knit 1, purl 1, across the whole row.
Row 2: Knit 1, purl 1, across the whole row.

Single twisted rib

This is worked like single rib, but all of the knit stitches are worked through the back loop.

Triple rib (3x3)

This is worked over 2 rows and a number of stitches equal to a multiple of 6:
Row 1: Knit 3, purl 3, across the whole row.
Row 2: Knit 3, purl 3, across the whole row.

Moss stitch

This stitch, made up of alternating single rib, is worked over 2 rows and an even number of stitches:
Row 1: Knit 1, purl 1, across the whole row.
Row 2: Purl 1, knit 1, across the whole row.

III - Increases

Yarn-over increase

To make a yarn-over increase, which creates a hole, you just need to wrap the yarn around the right needle, taking it from the back towards the front and upwards from below, then towards the back again, between two knit stitches.

In the next row, insert the right needle into the loop as if it were a stitch and work it normally (purl for a purl stitch, knit for a knit stitch).

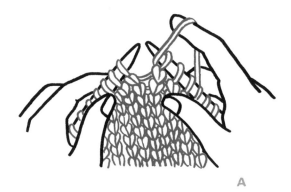

A

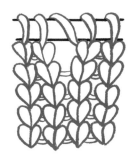

B

Make-one increase ('Make 1')

1. Insert the point of the left needle under the yarn of the previous row connecting the stitch you have just worked to the following stitch, from front to back (A).

2. With the right needle, knit the yarn through the back loop (B).

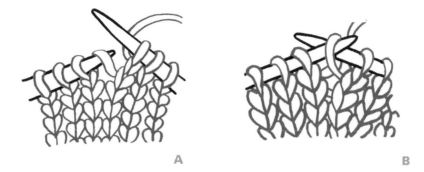

A   B

IV - Decreases

Slip-stitch-over decrease

1. Slip 1 stitch from the left needle onto the right needle, as when you are making a knit stitch, but without knitting it (A).

2. Knit the next stitch, then insert the point of the left needle into the slipped stitch, from left to right (B), lift the stitch up and over the knitted stitch (C).

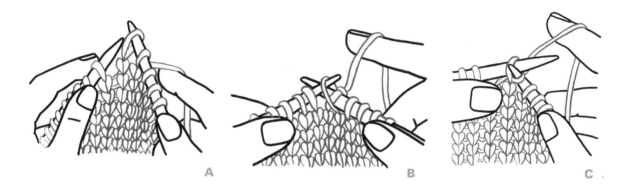

A   B   C

Knit 2 together

1. Insert the point of the right needle into 2 stitches at once, from left to right (A).

2. Knit these 2 stitches together as if they were 1 stitch.

A

How to make a buttonhole

Row 1: At the place you would like to make the buttonhole, cast off the desired number of stitches, then continue to work the row normally.

Row 2: Work the stitches until you reach the last stitch before the buttonhole, then cast back on as many stitches as you previously cast off and work the following stitches normally.

V - Other stitches

4-stitch left-twisting cable

Slip 2 stitches onto a double-pointed needle placed in front, knit the next 2 stitches (A), then pick back up the stitches on hold from the double-pointed needle and knit them (B).

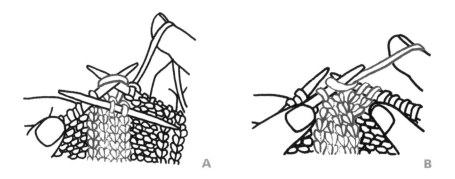

VI - To finish

Pick up and knit

1. Insert the point of the needle into the work from front to back, 1 stitch or 1 row inside the edge (A).

2. Wrap the yarn around the point of the needle (B).

3. Pull through the loop of yarn as if making 1 knit stitch, bringing it towards the front (C).

4. Repeat the process, making 1 stitch between each row, or each cast-off stitch (D).

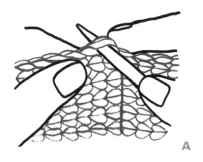
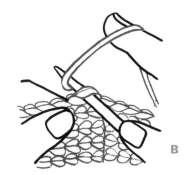

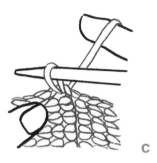

C

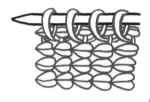

D

Mattress stitch seam

This is the ideal stitch for vertical seams.

A

B

Backstitch seam

This is the strongest stitch, and the easiest to do.

Cute as a button

The special feature of this pattern is that different sizes can be achieved by using smaller or larger knitting needles… For the 3–6 months size, use 2.75 mm (US 2/UK 12) needles; for the 9–12 months size, use 3 mm (US 2/UK 11) or even 3.5 mm (US 4/UK 10) needles.

SIZES: 3–6 months (9–12 months)

STITCH USED: Garter stitch (see p. 11)

10 x 10 CM (4 x 4 INCH) TENSION SQUARE IN GARTER STITCH: 24 stitches x 52 rows, using 2.75 mm (US 2/UK 12) needles

MATERIALS AND TOOLS
1 ball of alpaca wool in Papaya
One pair of 2.75 mm (US 2/UK 12) needles
1 stitch-holder or large safety pin
1 wool needle
2 velvet buttons

INSTRUCTIONS

For the bootie

Beginning at the sole, cast on 40 stitches and work in garter stitch as follows:

Row 1: Knit 1, make 1*, knit 18, make 1, knit 1, make 1, knit 1, make 1, knit 18, make 1, knit 1 = 45 stitches.

Row 2 (and every alternate row): Knit.

Row 3: Knit 2, make 1, knit 18, make 1, knit 2, make 1, knit 3, make 1, knit 18, make 1, knit 2 = 50 stitches.

Row 5: Knit 3, make 1, knit 18, make 1, knit 4, make 1, knit 4, make 1, knit 18, make 1, knit 3 = 55 stitches.

Row 7: Knit 4, make 1, knit 18, make 1, knit 5, make 1, knit 6, make 1, knit 18, make 1, knit 4 = 60 stitches.

Row 9: Knit 5, make 1, knit 18, make 1, knit 7, make 1, knit 7, make 1, knit 18, make 1, knit 5 = 65 stitches.

Row 11: Knit 24, make 1, knit 9, make 1, knit 8, make 1, knit 24 = 68 stitches.

Continue in garter stitch without shaping until you have worked 26 rows in total, or 13 'ridges'.

Row 27 (shape the instep): Knit 29, knit 2 together, knit 6, knit 2 together. Turn the work around and start working in the other direction as follows:

Next row: Slip 1 stitch onto the other needle without working it, knit 6, knit 2 together. Turn the work and start working in the other direction as follows:

Next row: Slip 1 stitch onto the other needle without working it, knit 6, knit 2 together. Turn the work again.

Repeat the last row until there are 20 stitches left on each side of the instep. Do not turn after the last decrease.

Work to the end of the row, knitting the remaining 20 stitches on the left needle.

Next row: Knit 19, knit 2 together, knit 6, knit 2 together, knit 19.

Next row: Knit 9, cast off the next 28 stitches, knit 9 (this includes 1 stitch already on the needle after cast off).

Place the remaining stitches on a stitch-holder.

Cut the yarn, leaving enough length to sew up the bootie.

For the strap

Transfer the 18 remaining stitches to one knitting needle and join in the yarn to the front edge (not the centre back).

Cast on 6 stitches at the beginning of the row, then knit across these stitches and the 18 stitches on the needle.

Next row: Cast on 10 stitches at the beginning of the row, then knit to the end of the row.

Work 4 rows in garter stitch and cast off.

Important: For the other bootie, you need to remember to reverse the direction of the strap, first casting on 10 stitches, then 6 stitches.

TO MAKE UP

Fold the bootie with right sides together and sew up the centre back and sole seam. Embroider a button loop on the long end of the strap. Sew the buttons on the opposite end of the strap to correspond with the loop. Darn in the yarn ends.

TIP

If you are not in an embroidering mood, replace the button loop and the button with a small press-stud.

---

* *'Make 1': To increase 1 stitch between 2 stitches, slip the point of the left needle under the strand in the previous row that connects the stitch you have just worked to the next one, from front to back. Then proceed as for a knit stitch, working the strand through the back loop (see p. 12).*

Sweet Mary Janes

Very chic Mary Janes to wear on special occasions…

Sizes: 3–6 months (9–12 months)

Stitch used: Moss stitch (see p.12)

10 x 10 cm (4 x 4 inch) tension square in moss stitch: 26 stitches x 42 rows, using 3 mm (US 2/UK 11) needles

Materials and tools
1 ball of pearl cotton yarn in Lilac
One pair of 3 mm (US 2/UK 11) needles
1 safetypin
1 wool needle
2 flower-shaped mother-of-pearl buttons

Instructions

For the bootie

Cast on 20 (24) stitches and work 1 row in moss stitch.

Rows 2, 4, 6 and 8: Increase 1 stitch at each end of the row, working in moss stitch = 28 (32) stitches.

Rows 3, 5, 7 and 9: Work in moss stitch.

Work a further 3 (5) rows in moss stitch, then, in every alternate row, decrease 1 stitch at each end (4 times) = 20 (24) stitches.

Next row: Work in moss stitch and cast on 8 (9) stitches after the last stitch in the row.

Next row: Continue in moss stitch, increase 1 stitch in the last stitch, then work 1 row in moss stitch. Repeat these 2 rows 4 (5) times = 33 (38) stitches.

Next row: Cast off 10 (12) stitches, work 3 stitches, cast off 4 stitches, work the 16 (19) remaining stitches.

Next row: Work 16 (19) stitches in moss stitch and place the 3 other stitches on hold on a safety pin.

Work 10 (12) rows in moss stitch.

Next row: Work 16 (19) stitches, then cast on 17 (19) stitches.

Next row and all remaining rows: Continue in moss stitch, decreasing 1 stitch at the rounded end every 2 rows (5 (6) times), then cast off all remaining stitches.

For the strap

Pick up the 3 stitches on hold and increase 1 stitch in the 1st and 2nd stitch = 5 stitches.

Work 15 (17) rows in moss stitch.

Next row: For the buttonhole, work 2 stitches, cast off the 3rd stitch, then work the next 2 stitches.

Next row: Work 2 stitches, cast on 1 stitch after the 2nd stitch, work 2 stitches.

Work 4 rows in moss stitch, then cast off the 5 stitches.

To make up

Sew up the heel and the side of the sole. Pin the top part of the foot around the end of the sole and sew it up. Darn in the ends and sew on a small mother-of-pearl button to correspond with the strap.

Important: The other bootie is made in the same way but, when making it up, you need to sew it up the opposite way so that you make a left foot and a right foot.

Remember to sew on the button very tightly, and to check the button remains secure after washing.

Norwegian socks

*A traditional jacquard motif gives a Scandinavian touch
to these super-comfortable socks, made in a two- or three-colour pattern,
and decorated, if you like, with little pompoms (see next page).*

Sizes: 3–6 months (9–12 months)

Stitches used: Stocking stitch (see p. 11), single rib
(see p. 12), jacquard pattern, garter stitch (see p. 11)

**10 x 10 cm (4 x 4 inch) tension square in
stocking stitch:** 30 stitches x 32 rows, using 3 mm
(US 2/UK 11) needles

Materials and tools
1 ball of pure wool in Pearl Grey
1 ball of pure wool in Lavender Blue
1 ball of pure wool in Azure Blue
One pair of 3 mm (US 2/UK 11) needles
1 wool needle

Instructions

Begin at the ankle

Cast on 38 (44) stitches in Pearl Grey yarn and work 3 (5) rows
in single rib, then 1 row in purl. (For the 9–12 months size,
work an extra 2 rows in stocking stitch).

Work the next rows following the jacquard chart, starting
at the coloured motif (Row 1). To keep the motifs centred,
mark the centre stitch on your chart and adjust the number of
stitches on either side to correspond to the stitches on your
needle. Work the 1st motif in Lavender, the 2nd in Azure and
the 3rd in Lavender, stopping at the end of the 5th (7th) row of
the chart, that is, at the end of the 19th (21st) row of jacquard
= 23 (29) rows in all.

Shape the instep

Row 24 (30): Purl 25 (29) in Pearl Grey, turn the work around
and knit 12 (14). Turn the work around again.

Keeping the jacquard pattern correct (one Azure motif, one
Lavender motif) continue on these 12 (14) centre stitches
(leaving 13 (15) stitches on the needle at each end) and work
15 rows of stocking stitch.

Next row (shape toe): Knit 2 together, knit 8 (10), knit
2 together.

Next row: Purl 2 together, purl 6 (8), purl 2 together.

Next row: Knit 2 together, knit 4 (6), knit 2 together. Cut the
yarn. With the wrong side of the work facing you, transfer
these 6 (8) stitches onto the right-hand needle, next to the
13 (15) stitches already on hold on that needle.

Join in the Pearl Grey yarn to the 13 (15) stitches on the
other needle and purl them.

Shape the sides

Next row: Knit 13 (15), then pick up and knit 14 (16) stitches
along the selvedge of the instep, knit the 6 (8) stitches at the
toe end of the foot, pick up and knit 14 (16) stitches along the
second selvedge of the instep, then knit the 13 (15) remaining
stitches = 60 (70) stitches.

Work a further 9 (13) rows in garter stitch.

Shape the sole

Row 11 (15): Knit 2, knit 2 together, knit 22 (27), knit 2
together, knit 4, knit 2 together, knit 22 (27), knit 2 together,
knit 2.

Row 12 (16): Knit.

Row 13 (17): Knit 2, knit 2 together, knit 20 (25), knit 2
together, knit 4, knit 2 together, knit 20 (25), knit 2 together,
knit 2.

Row 14 (18): Knit.

Row 15 (19): Knit 2, knit 2 together, knit 18 (23), knit 2
together, knit 4, knit 2 together, knit 18 (23), knit 2 together,
knit 2.

Row 16 (20): Knit.

Row 17 (21): Knit 2, knit 2 together, knit 16 (19), knit 2
together, knit 4, knit 2 together, knit 16 (19), knit 2 together,
knit 2.

Row 18 (22): Cast off all remaining stitches.

To make up

Sew up the sole and centre backseam on the wrong side of
the work, 1 stitch inside the edge. Darn in all the ends on the
wrong side of the work.

Make the second sock in the same way.

Jacquard chart

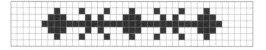

Pompom socks

This charming pair features the same jacquard motif as the Norwegian socks, but the pompoms make all the difference.

SIZES: 3–6 months (9–12 months)

STITCHES USED: Stocking stitch (see p. 11), single rib (see p. 12), jacquard pattern (see p. 21), garter stitch (see p. 11)

10 x 10 CM (4 x 4 INCH) TENSION SQUARE IN STOCKING STITCH: 30 stitches x 32 rows, using 3 mm (US 2/UK 11) needles

MATERIALS AND TOOLS
1 ball of pure wool in Pearl Grey
1 ball of pure wool in Midnight Blue
One pair of 3 mm (US 2/UK 11) needles
1 wool needle
2 rounds of cardboard, 3 cm (1¼ inch) in diameter, with a hole in the middle

INSTRUCTIONS

Begin at the ankle

Cast on 38 (44) stitches in Pearl Grey yarn and work 3 (5) rows in single rib, then 1 row in purl. (For the 9–12 months size, work an extra 2 rows in stocking stitch).

Work the next rows following the jacquard chart (on page 21), starting at the coloured motif (Row 1). To keep the motifs centred, mark the centre stitch on your chart and adjust the number of stitches on either side to correspond to the stitches on your needle. Work 3 jacquard motifs in Midnight Blue, stopping at the end of the 5th (7th) row of the chart after motif 3, that is, at the end of the 19th (21st) row of jacquard = 23 (29) rows in all.

Shape the instep

Row 24 (30): Purl 25 (29) in Pearl Grey, turn the work around and knit 12 (14). Turn the work around again.

Keeping the jacquard pattern correct, continue on these 12 (14) centre stitches (leaving 13 (15) stitches on the needle at each end) and work 15 rows of stocking stitch.

Next row (shape toe): Knit 2 together, knit 8 (10), knit 2 together.

Next row: Purl 2 together, purl 6 (8), purl 2 together.

Next row: Knit 2 together, knit 4 (6), knit 2 together. Cut the yarn. With the wrong side of the work facing you, transfer these 6 (8) stitches onto the right-hand needle, next to the 13 (15) stitches already on hold on that needle.

Join in the Pearl Grey yarn to the 13 (15) stitches on the other needle and purl them.

Shape the sides

Next row: Join in the Midnight Blue yarn and knit 13 (15), then pick up and knit 14 (16) stitches along the selvedge of the instep, knit the 6 (8) stitches at the toe end of the foot, pick up and knit 14 (16) stitches along the second selvedge of the instep, then knit the 13 (15) remaining stitches = 60 (70) stitches.

Work a further 9 (13) rows in garter stitch.

Shape the sole

Row 11 (15): Knit 2, knit 2 together, knit 22 (27), knit 2 together, knit 4, knit 2 together, knit 22 (27), knit 2 together, knit 2.

Row 12 (16): Knit.

Row 13 (17): Knit 2, knit 2 together, knit 20 (25), knit 2 together, knit 4, knit 2 together, knit 20 (25), knit 2 together, knit 2.

Row 14 (18): Knit.

Row 15 (19): Knit 2, knit 2 together, knit 18 (23), knit 2 together, knit 4, knit 2 together, knit 18 (23), knit 2 together, knit 2.

Row 16 (20): Knit.

Row 17 (21): Knit 2, knit 2 together, knit 16 (19), knit 2 together, knit 4, knit 2 together, knit 16 (19), knit 2 together, knit 2.

Row 18 (22): Cast off all remaining stitches.

TO MAKE UP

Sew up the sole and centre backseam on the wrong side of the work, 1 stitch inside the edge. Darn in all the ends on the wrong side of the work.

Make two pompoms, 3 cm (1¼ inch) in diameter, in Midnight Blue yarn (see p. 41), and a 6-strand cord (see below). Thread the cord through the ribbing at the top of the sock, beginning in the middle front of the leg, and weaving the cord in and out every 3 stitches. Sew a pompom to each end of the cord.

Make the second sock in the same way.

TIP

How to make a cord

Take 6 strands of wool, 3 times the desired final length of the cord, then tie a knot at each end of the bunch. Hook one end on something, pull the wool straight and slip a pencil or pen behind the knot in your hand. Keeping the yarn taut, turn the pencil around in one direction until the strands of wool are completely twisted, then unhook the end of the cord and allow the cord to twist back on itself from the mid point. Remove the pencil and, once the cord has finished twisting, knot the ends, 6 cm (2½ inch) from each end. Gently straighten out any kinks.

Pretty picot

Generally, socks are knitted using four needles, to avoid having a seam.
Here is a much simpler pattern, made using only two needles.
Make sure you use very fine stitches to sew up the seams.

SIZES: 3–6 months (9–12 months)

STITCH USED: Stocking stitch (see p. 11)

10 x 10 CM (4 x 4 INCH) TENSION SQUARE IN STOCKING STITCH: 30 stitches x 40 rows, using 3 mm (US 2/UK 11) needles

MATERIALS AND TOOLS
1 ball of pure wool in Powder Pink
One pair of 3 mm (US 2/UK 11) needles
1 wool needle
2 safety pins

INSTRUCTIONS

Begin at the ankle

Cast on 36 (40 stitches) loosely and work 4 rows in stocking stitch.

Row 5 (picot hemline): Knit 1, *knit 2 together, 1 yarn-over increase; repeat from * to the last 2 stitches, knit 2.

Row 6 and all even rows: Purl.

Work 10 (12) rows in stocking stitch.

Row 17 (19): Knit 5, knit 2 together, knit 22 (26), 1 slip-stitch-over decrease, knit 5 = 34 (38) stitches.

Work 5 (7) rows in stocking stitch.

Row 23 (27): Knit 4, knit 2 together, knit 22 (26), 1 slip-stitch-over decrease, knit 5 = 32 (36) stitches.

Work 3 (5) rows in stocking stitch.

Next row 27 (33): Knit 3, then [knit 2 together, knit 6 (7)] 3 times, knit 2 together, knit 3 (4) = 28 (32) stitches.

Shape the heel

Next row: Purl 8 (9), then turn the work.

Work these 8 (9) stitches in stocking stitch for 9 rows.

Next row: Purl 2 (3), purl 2 together, purl 1, turn the work.

Next row: Slip 1 stitch, knit 3 (4).

Next row: Purl 3 (4), purl 2 together, purl 1, turn the work.

Next row: Slip 1 stitch, knit 4 (5).

Next row: Purl 4 (5), purl 2 together.

Cut the yarn, leaving a generous length, and place these 5 (6) stitches on hold on a safety pin.

Working with the wrong side of the work facing you, place the first 12 (14) stitches on the needle onto another safety pin.

Join in the yarn and purl the next 8 (9) stitches.

Work 8 rows in stocking stitch.

Next row: Knit 2 (3), 1 slip-stitch-over decrease, knit 1, turn.

Next row: Slip 1 stitch, purl 3 (4).

Next row: Knit 3 (4), 1 slip-stitch-over decrease, knit 1, turn.

Next row: Slip 1 stitch, purl 4 (5).

Next row: Knit 4 (5), 1 slip-stitch-over decrease, turn.

Next row: Slip 1 stitch, purl 4 (5).

continued...

Shape the instep and side of foot

Knit 5 (6), pick up 8 stitches along the selvedge of the heel, pick up and knit the 12 (14) stitches on hold, pick up 8 stitches along the second inside selvedge of the heel, pick up and knit the 5 (6) stitches on hold on the other safety pin = 38 (42) stitches.

Purl all stitches in the next and every following alternate row.

Next row: Knit 11 (12), knit 2 together, knit 12 (14), 1 slip-stitch-over decrease, knit 11 (12).

Next row: Knit 10 (11), knit 2 together, knit 12 (14), 1 slip-stitch-over decrease, knit 10 (11).

Next row: Knit 9 (10), knit 2 together, knit 12 (14), 1 slip-stitch-over decrease, knit 9 (10) knit stitches.

Next row: Knit 8 (9), knit 2 together, knit 12 (14), 1 slip-stitch-over decrease, knit 8 (9) = 30 (34) stitches.

Work 15 (19) rows in stocking stitch.

Shape the toe

Next row: Knit 1, [1 slip-stitch-over decrease, knit 5 (6)] 4 times, knit 1 = 26 (30) stitches.

Purl all stitches in the next and every following alternate row.

Next row: Knit 1, [1 slip-stitch-over decrease, knit 4 (5)] 4 times, knit 1.

Next row: Knit 1, [1 slip-stitch-over decrease, knit 3 (4)] 4 times, knit 1.

Next row: Knit 1, [1 slip-stitch-over decrease, knit 2 (3)] 4 times, knit 1.

(For 9–12 months size only:

Purl all stitches in the next row.

Next row: Knit 1, [1 slip-stitch-over decrease, knit 2 together] 4 times, knit 1.)

For both sizes:

Next row: (Purl 2 together) 7 times.

TO MAKE UP

Cut the yarn, leaving a good length, thread it onto the wool needle, then thread it through the 7 remaining stitches and pull up tightly to close the end of the sock. Sew the foot and leg seam; fold over the picot edging around the top and slip-stitch it in place on the wrong side.

Make the second sock in the same way.

For every Princess

Mum, big sister and baby (or bunny) will appreciate the ultra-comfort of these booties and their fun shape, a nod to the stockings of the Middle Ages!

For baby

SIZES: 3–6 months (9–12 months)

STITCHES USED: Garter stitch (see p. 11) and stocking stitch (see p. 11)

10 x 10 MM (4 x 4 INCH) TENSION SQUARE IN STOCKING STITCH: 23 stitches x 33 rows, using 3.5 mm (US 4/UK 10) needles

MATERIALS AND TOOLS
1 ball of merino wool in Raspberry
One pair of 3.5 mm (US 4/UK 10) needles
One pair of 3 mm (US 2/UK 11) needles
1 wool needle

INSTRUCTIONS

For the sole, in garter stitch

Cast on 16 (17) stitches on the 3.5 mm (US 4/UK 10) needles, work 1 row in knit.

Row 2: Increase once in the first stitch, then knit to the end of the row.

Row 3: Knit.

Rows 4 and 6: As for Row 2.

Rows 5 and 7: As for Row 3.

Rows 8 and 9: Knit.

(**For the 9–12 months size**: Work an extra 2 rows, not included in the row count below).

Rows 10, 12 and 14: Knit 2 together, then knit to the end of the row.

Rows 11, 13 and 15: Knit.

For the top of the bootie, in stocking stitch

Row 16: Cast on 6 (7) stitches at the beginning of the row, then knit to the end of the row.

Row 17: Knit 2, make 1, then knit the remaining 20 (22) stitches.

Row 18: Purl.

Row 19: Knit 2, make 1, then knit the remaining 21 (23) stitches.

Row 20: Purl.

Row 21: Knit 2, make 1, then knit the remaining 22 (24) stitches.

Row 22: Cast off the first 12 (13) stitches loosely, and purl the remaining 13 (14) stitches.

(**For the 9–12 months size**: Work an extra 2 rows in stocking stitch, not included in the row count below).

Row 23: Knit.

Row 24: Cast on 12 (13) stitches at the beginning of the row, then purl 22 (24), purl 2 together, purl 1.

Rows 25, 27 and 29: Knit.

Row 26: Purl 21 (23), purl 2 together, purl 1.

Row 28: Purl 20 (22), purl 2 together, purl 1.

Row 30: Cast off all remaining stitches.

TO MAKE UP

Using the 3 mm (US 2/UK 11) needles, pick up 25 (27) stitches around the ankle. With the right side of the work facing you, work 7 rows in stocking stitch, then cast off the stitches very loosely.

Sew up the back of the ankle and around the sole.

Make the second bootie in the same way.

continued...

For an older child

SIZE: To fit a 13 cm (5 inch) foot

STITCHES USED: Garter stitch (see p. 11) and stocking stitch (see p. 11)

10 x 10 CM (4 x 4 INCH) TENSION SQUARE IN STOCKING STITCH: 23 stitches x 33 rows, using 3.5 mm (US 4/UK 10) needles

INSTRUCTIONS

For the sole, in garter stitch

Cast on 19 stitches on the 3.5 mm (US 4/UK 10) needles, knit 2 rows, then increase 2 stitches at each end of the 3rd row = 23 stitches.

Rows 4, 6 and 8: Knit.

Rows 5 and 7: Increase 1 stitch in the first and last stitch of the row.

Work 10 rows in garter stitch.

Row 19: Knit 2 together, knit 23, knit 2 together. Knit all stitches in the return row.

Row 21: Knit 2 together, knit 21, knit 2 together. Knit all stitches in the return row.

Row 23: Knit 2 together, knit 19, knit 2 together. Knit all stitches in the return row.

For the top of the bootie, in stocking stitch

Row 1: Cast on 7 stitches for the heel at the beginning of

MATERIALS AND TOOLS
1 ball of merino wool in Turquoise Blue
One pair of 3.5 mm (US 4/UK 10) needles
One pair of 3 mm (US 2/UK 11) needles
1 wool needle

the row, then work in stocking stitch, increasing 1 stitch at 3 stitches in from the left edge of this row.

Continue in stocking stitch, repeating this increase 6 times, every 2 rows (= 7 increases in all).

Row 13: Cast off 15 stitches on the right for one side of ankle.

Rows 21, 23, 25, 27, 29, 31, 33: Knit 2 together at 2 stitches in from the left edge, every 2 rows.

At the same time, in Row 22, increase by 15 stitches with the right side facing you, for the other side of the ankle.

Row 35: Cast off all remaining stitches.

TO MAKE UP

Using the 3 mm (US 2/UK 11) needles, pick up 40 stitches around the ankle. With the right side facing you, work 8 rows in stocking stitch, then cast off the stitches very loosely. Sew up the back of the ankle and around the sole.

Make the second bootie in the same way.

For mum

SIZE: To fit a 25 cm (10 inch) foot

STITCHES USED: Garter stitch (see p. 11) and stocking stitch (see p. 11)

10 x 10 CM (4 x 4 INCH) TENSION SQUARE IN STOCKING STITCH: 23 stitches x 33 rows, using 3.5 mm (US 4/UK 10) needles

INSTRUCTIONS

For the sole, in garter stitch

Cast on 32 stitches on the 3.5 mm (US 4/UK 10) needles and knit 2 rows.

Row 3: Cast on 2 stitches at the beginning of the row, knit to the end of the row, then turn the work and cast on 2 stitches = 36 stitches.

Row 4 and all even rows of the sole: Knit.

Rows 5 and 7: Cast on 2 stitches at the beginning of the row, knit to the end of the row, then turn the work and cast on 2 stitches.

Row 9: Cast on 1 stitch at the begininng of the row, knit to the end of the row, then turn the work and cast on 1 stitch = 46 stitches.

Work 22 rows in garter stitch (or 11 ridges).

Next row: Knit 2 together, knit 42, knit 2 together. Purl all stitches in the return row.

Next row: Cast off 2 stitches, knit to the end of the row.

Repeat the last row 5 more times = 32 stitches.

Knit 2 rows.

For the top of the foot, in stocking stitch

Row 1: Cast on 16 stitches at the beginning of the row, knit

MATERIALS AND TOOLS
1 ball of merino wool in Denim Blue
One pair of 3.5 mm (US 4/UK 10) needles
One pair of 3 mm (US 2/UK 11) needles
1 wool needle

these stitches, then knit 29, make 1, knit 3.

Row 2 and all even rows: Purl.

Odd rows: Knit, increasing1 stitch at 3 stitches in from the left edge every 2 rows (8 times) = 9 increases in total.

Next row: Purl.

Next row: Cast off 25 stitches, knit to the end of the row.

Next row: Purl.

Continue in stocking stitch for 8 rows, casting on 25 stitches at the beginning of the 5th row.

Next row: Knit, knitting 2 together at 2 stitches in from the left edge.

Work stocking stitch, repeating this decrease every 2 rows a further 8 times = 9 decreases. Purl all stitches in the return row.

Next row: Cast off all remaining stitches.

TO MAKE UP

Using the 3 mm (US 2/UK 11) needles, pick up 56 stitches around the ankle. With the right side facing you, work 12 rows in stocking stitch. Cast off the stitches very loosely, then sew up the back of the ankle and around the sole.

Make the second bootie in the same way.

Tweed espadrilles

Soft linen yarn in a tweedy weave is used to make these simple slippers for lively little feet.

SIZES: 3–6 months (9–12 months)

STITCH USED: Garter stitch (see p. 11)

10 x 10 CM (4 x 4 INCH) TENSION SQUARE IN GARTER STITCH: 23 stitches x 33 rows, using 3.5 mm (US 4/UK 10) needles

INSTRUCTIONS

Cast on 22 (26) stitches and work 4 (4.5) cm (1½/ 1¾ inch) in garter stitch.
Next row, cast off 10 (12) stitches and work on the 12 (14) remaining stitches for another 3 (3.5) cm (1¼/ 1½ inch).
Cast on 10 (12) stitches, and work on these 22 (26) stitches for another 4 (4.5) cm (1½/ 1¾ inch). Cast off all remaining stitches.

MATERIALS AND TOOLS

1 ball of tweed linen yarn in Denim Blue
One pair of 3.5 mm (US 4/UK 10) needles
1 wool needle
40 cm (16 inch) indigo silk cord (or 2 x 20 cm (8 inch))
1 reel of Indigo thread
1 sewing needle

TO MAKE UP

Sew up the sole by sewing together the starting and finishing rows. Sew up the back of the heel. Next, thread a drawstring through the open end of the bootie and pull up tightly to close the toe. Cut the silk cord in half. Sew the mid-point of a silk cord at the top of the heel seam, using small, strong stitches in Indigo thread.

Make the second bootie in the same way.

La vie en rose

A cloud of pink with a lacy edging — irresistible!

SIZES: 3–6 months (9–12 months)

STITCHES USED: Garter stitch (see p. 11), stocking stitch (see p. 11), single twisted rib (see p. 12), diamond edge (see below)

10 x 10 CM (4 x 4 INCH) TENSION SQUARE IN GARTER STITCH: 28 stitches x 46 rows, using 3 mm (US 2/UK 11) needles

MATERIALS AND TOOLS
1 ball of lambswool in Dusty Pink
One pair of 3 mm (US 2/UK 11) needles
1 wool needle

INSTRUCTIONS

Beginning at the ruffle edge, cast on 49 (61) stitches.

Row 1: *Knit 1, 1 yarn-over increase, knit 4, slip 1 stitch, knit 2 together, pass slipped stitch over, knit 4, 1 yarn-over increase**, repeat from * to ** to last stitch, knit 1.

Row 2 and all even rows: Knit.

Row 3: *Knit 2, 1 yarn-over increase, knit 3, slip 1 stitch, knit 2 together, pass slipped stitch over, knit 3, 1 yarn-over increase, knit 1**, repeat from * to ** to last stitch, knit 1.

Row 5: *Knit 3, 1 yarn-over increase, knit 2, slip 1 stitch, knit 2 together, pass slipped stitch over, knit 2, 1 yarn-over increase, knit 2**, repeat from * to ** to last stitch, knit 1.

Row 7: *Knit 4, 1 yarn-over increase, knit 1, slip 1 stitch, knit 2 together, pass slipped stitch over, knit 1, 1 yarn-over increase, knit 3**, repeat from * to ** to last stitch, knit 1.

Row 9: *Knit 5, slip 1 stitch, knit 2 together, pass slipped stitch over, knit 4**, repeat from * to ** to last stitch, knit 1.

Row 10: *Purl 2 together, purl 8**, repeat from * to ** to last stitch, purl 1. There should be 37 (46) stitches remaining.

Work 7 rows in single twisted rib.

Row 18: Knit 1, *knit 1, 1 yarn-over increase, knit 2 together**, repeat from * to ** to end of row (finish with knit 1 for the 9–12 months size).

Work 3 rows in stocking stitch, beginning with a purl row.

For the instep

Knit 25 (31), turn the work around, place the next 12 (15) stitches on hold and purl the next 13 (16) stitches, turn the work around and once again place 12 (15) stitches on hold. Work 4 (6) rows of stocking stitch across the middle 13 (16) stitches.

Proceed on the centre stitches, as follows, for heart motif:

Row 1: Knit 4 (5), purl 2, knit 1 (2), purl 2, knit 4 (5).

Row 2: Purl 3 (4), knit 3, purl 1 (2), knit 3, purl 3 (4).

Rows 3 and 5: Knit 3 (4), purl 7 (8), knit 3 (4).

Row 4: Purl 3 (4), knit 7 (8), purl 3 (4).

Row 6: Purl 4 (5), knit 5 (6), purl 4 (5).

Row 7: Knit 4 (5), purl 5 (6), knit 4 (5).

Row 8: Purl 5 (6), knit 3 (4), purl 5 (6).

Row 9: Knit 5 (6), purl 3 (4), knit 5 (6).

Row 10: Purl 6 (7), knit 1 (2), purl 6 (7).

Work 4 (6) rows in stocking stitch. Cut the yarn.

Join in yarn and knit the first 12 (15) stitches placed on hold, pick up 13 (15) stitches along the selvedge of the instep, work across 13 (16) stitches of the instep, pick up 13 (15) stitches along the second selvedge, and knit the last 12 (15) stitches placed on hold = 63 (76) stitches.

Work 11 (15) rows in garter stitch (all knit).

For the sole, size 3–6 months

Row 1: Knit 1, knit 2 together, knit 26, knit 2 together, knit 1, knit 2 together, knit 26, knit 2 together, knit 1.

Rows 2 and 4: Knit 1, knit 2 together, knit to the last 3 stitches, knit 2 together, knit 1.

Row 3: Knit 1, knit 2 together, knit 23, knit 2 together, knit 1, knit 2 together, knit 23, knit 2 together, knit 1.

Row 5: Knit 1, knit 2 together, knit 20, knit 2 together, knit 1, knit 2 together, knit 20, knit 2 together, knit 1.

Row 6: Cast off all stitches loosely.

For the sole, size 9–12 months

Row 1: Knit 1, knit 2 together, knit 33, knit 2 together (twice), knit 33, knit 2 together, knit 1.

Rows 2 and 4: Knit 1, knit 2 together, knit to the last 3 stitches, knit 2 together, knit 1.

Row 3: Knit 1, knit 2 together, knit 30, knit 2 together (twice), knit 30, knit 2 together, knit 1.

Row 5: Knit 1, knit 2 together, knit 27, knit 2 together (twice), knit 27, knit 2 together, knit 1.

Row 6: Cast off all stitches loosely.

TO MAKE UP

Sew up the underside of the sole and the leg, to the top of the sides. Make a cord (see p. 22) and thread it through the eyelets of the work, so it can be tied at the front or back. Make sure the cord is tied tightly, so your baby cannot undo the knot.

Soft as cashmere

There is nothing better than cashmere for keeping baby's neck and little feet warm

Scarf

MATERIALS AND TOOLS
1 ball of cashmere yarn in Mauve (A)
1 ball of cashmere yarn in Lilac (B)
1 ball of cashmere yarn in Purple (C)
1 ball of cashmere yarn in Blue-grey (D)
One pair of 4 mm (US 6/UK 8) knitting needles
1 wool needle

ONE SIZE

STITCHES USED: Garter stitch (see p. 11) and triple rib (see p. 12)

10 x 10 CM (4 x 4 INCH) TENSION SQUARE IN TRIPLE RIB: 24 stitches x 26 rows (piece lightly flattened using a damp ironing cloth), using 4 mm (US 6/UK 8) needles

INSTRUCTIONS

Cast on 27 stitches in yarn colour D.

Work 4 rows triple rib in yarn D, 4 rows in yarn C, 4 rows in yarn B, 4 rows in yarn A, 4 rows in yarn B, 4 rows in yarn C, and so on, taking care, with each change of colour, to leave a maximum length of 2 to 3 cm (¾ to 1¼ inch) when cutting the two strands and knotting them together (cashmere is expensive, no need to waste lengths of it). Continue, following the same order of colours.

When the work measures 58 cm (23 inches) from the beginning, cast off the stitches.

Next, cast on 140 stitches in yarn colour A on each side of the scarf, work 4 rows in garter stitch and cast off.

Cast on 32 stitches in yarn D at each end, work 4 rows in garter stitch and cast off all remaining stitches.

Darn in all of the yarn ends.

continued...

Booties

SIZES: 3–6 months (9–12 months)

STITCH USED: Stocking stitch (see p. 11)

10 x 10 CM (4 x 4 INCH) TENSION SQUARE IN STOCKING STITCH: 20 stitches x 32 rows, using 3.5 mm (US 4/UK 10) needles

MATERIALS AND TOOLS

Cashmere yarn left over from scarf
One pair of 3.5 mm (US 4/UK 10) knitting needles
1 wool needle
50 cm (20 inch) thin fancy ribbon or leather shoelace.

INSTRUCTIONS

Bootie sole (make 2)

Cast on 34 (38) stitches in yarn colour D.

Row 1: Purl.

Row 2: Knit 1, make 1, knit 15 (17), make 1, knit 2, make 1, knit 15 (17), make 1, knit 1.

Row 3: Purl.

Row 4: Knit 2, make 1, knit 15 (17), make 1, knit 4, make 1, knit 15 (17), make 1, knit 2.

Row 5: Purl.

(For the 9–12 months size only:

Row 6: Knit 3, make 1, knit 15 (17), make 1, knit 6, make 1, knit 15 (17), make 1, knit 3.

Row 7: Purl.)

For both sizes: To shape the sole, work in purl with the right side of the work facing you: purl 12 (14), cast off the next 18 (22) stitches, working them purlwise, purl 12 (14).

Next, work 12 (14) stitches for one side, in striped stocking stitch (as follows), placing the remaining stitches on hold:

Rows 1 and 4: Yarn C.

Rows 2 and 5: Yarn B.

Rows 3 and 6: Yarn A.

Row 7: Cast off 12 (14) stitches purlwise.

Pick back up the 12 (14) remaining stitches and work them in the same way, then cast off.

Bootie upper (make 2)

Cast on 18 (22) stitches in yarn colour D and work 13 (16) rows of stocking stitch

Row 14 (17): Keeping the stocking stitch pattern correct, work 2 stitches together across the whole row.

Cut the yarn then thread it through the 9 (11) remaining stitches, pull up tightly and knot securely.

TO MAKE UP

Sew up the middle of the sole and the back of the foot. Sew the top of the bootie to the sole. Thread the ribbon through the knitted fabric, between two stitches, along the sides and across the top of the bootie, leaving a length at the back so it can be tied around the ankle.

PLEASE NOTE:

Make sure you double-knot the ties on these booties so that they are secure and your baby can't undo the knot and remove the ribbon. Loose or dangling ties could be unsafe.

Tricksy pixie

Two little pompoms and voilà — a very simple pair of booties is transformed into little pixie boots.

SIZES: 3–6 months (9–12 months)

STITCH USED: Garter stitch (see p. 11)

10 x 10 CM (4 x 4 INCH) TENSION SQUARE IN GARTER STITCH: 30 stitches x 32 rows, using 2.75 mm (US 2/UK 12) needles

INSTRUCTIONS

Cast on 60 (70) stitches and work 30 (34) rows in garter stitch, then cast off 20 (23) stitches at each end. Continue working the remaining 20 (24) stitches for 8 rows, then cast off all remaining stitches.

TO MAKE UP

Fold the piece of knitting in half and sew the sole seam, then the toe end of the foot (pulling the thread slightly to shape the toe), then the instep, up to the band formed by the middle stitches. Fold this band over on itself, to make the cuff. Make a cord using 2 strands of wool (see p. 22). Slip it under the fold of the cuff, then sew up the cuff, using running stitch, matching stitch to stitch.

Make the second bootie in the same way

Make two pompoms, 2 cm (¾ inch) in diameter. Sew them onto the gathered sections at the toes of the booties.

MATERIALS AND TOOLS
1 ball of pure wool in Mauve
One pair of 2.75 mm (US 2/UK 12) needles
1 wool needle
2 rounds of cardboard, 2 cm (¾ inch) in diameter, with a hole in the middle

TIP

How to make a pompom

Place the two rounds of cardboard on top of one other, and wrap wool around them until the centre hole is completely full. Next, insert the point of a pair of scissors between the two cardboard circles and cut the wool all around the circle, holding it firmly in one hand. Slip a piece of wool about 30 cm (12 inches) long between the two circles, pull tightly and make a double-knot before removing the two pieces of cardboard. Fluff up the pompom and trim if necessary.

Tiny dancer

Soft silk knitted to make the sweetest ballet slippers and a matching pouch.

Gift pouch

ONE SIZE

STITCHES USED: Garter stitch (see p. 11) and stocking stitch (see p. 11)

10 x 10 CM (4 x 4 INCH) TENSION SQUARE IN GARTER STITCH: 30 stitches x 42 rows, using 2.75 mm (US 2/UK 12) needles

INSTRUCTIONS

Cast on 64 stitches and work 8 rows in garter stitch.

Work the next 22 rows as follows: work the first 4 and last 4 stitches of each row in garter stitch, and the middle 56 stitches in stocking stitch.

In the 2nd row of stocking stitch, make 3 buttonholes, each 2 stitches wide (see p. 14): the first one 12 stitches from the edge, the second one 17 stitches from the first, and the third one 17 stitches after the second. Work the remaining 12 stitches to finish the row.

MATERIALS AND TOOLS
1 ball of silk yarn in Pearl Pink
One pair of 2.75 mm (US 2/UK 12) needles
1 wool needle
3 small mother-of-pearl buttons

Next, work 26 cm (10½ inches) entirely in stocking stitch, without the edging in garter stitch. Cast off all remaining stitches.

TO MAKE UP

Sew up the sides of the pouch on the wrong side of the work, then sew on the three buttons to correspond with the buttonholes. Iron on a very cool setting.

Little ballet slippers

SIZES: 3–6 months (9–12 months)

STITCHES USED: Garter stitch (see p. 11) and reverse stocking stitch (see p. 11)

10 x 10 CM (4 x 4 INCH) TENSION SQUARE IN GARTER STITCH: 28 stitches and 50 rows, using 2.75 mm (US 2/UK 12) needles

INSTRUCTIONS

Cast on 22 (26) stitches in Dusty Pink and knit 1 row.

Row 2: Knit, increasing 1 stitch at each end of the row = 24 (28) stitches.

Rows 3, 5, 7 and 9: Knit.

Rows 4, 6, 8 and 10: Knit, increasing 1 stitch at each end of the row = 32 (36) stitches.

Row 11: Knit.

Rows 12, 14, 16, 18 and 20: Knit 2 together, knit to the last 2 stitches, knit 2 together = 22 (26) stitches.

Rows 13, 15, 17 and 19: Knit.

Row 21: Knit to end of row.

Row 22: Cast on 5 (6) stitches at the beginning of the row, then knit to the end of the row = 27 (32) stitches.

Row 23: Increase 1 stitch at the beginning of the row, then knit to the end of the row.

Rows 24, 25, 26: Knit.

Rows 27, 31, 35, 39: Increase 1 stitch at the beginning of the row, then knit to the end of the row.

MATERIALS AND TOOLS
1 ball of silk yarn in Dusty Pink
Pearl Pink silk yarn left over from the gift pouch
One pair of 2.75 mm (US 2/UK 12) needles
1 wool needle

Rows 28, 29, 30, 32, 33, 34, 36, 37, 38, 40: Knit.

Row 41: Knit all 32 (37) stitches.

(For the 9–12 months size only: Work a further 2 rows, increasing 1 stitch at the beginning of the first row.)

Row 42 (44): Cast off 20 (22) stitches, then knit to the last stitch, and make 1 increase = 13 (17) stitches.

Rows 43 to 53 (45 to 59): Knit.

Row 54 (60): Cast on 20 (22) stitches at the beginning of the row then knit to the end of the row = 33 (39) stitches.

Rows 55, 59, 63, 67 (63, 67, 71, 75): Knit 2 together, then knit to the end of the row.

Rows 56, 57, 58, 60, 61, 62, 64, 65,66, 68 (61, 62, 64, 65,66, 68, 69, 70, 72, 73, 74, 76): Knit.

Cast off all stitches.

TO MAKE UP

Pick up 48 stitches around the ankle in Pearl Pink yarn. Work 1 row of reverse stocking stitch and cast off the stitches in the next row. Sew up bootie on wrong side of work, beginning with the heel, then sew the sole seam. Darn in the ends and turn right side out. Make a second bootie the same.

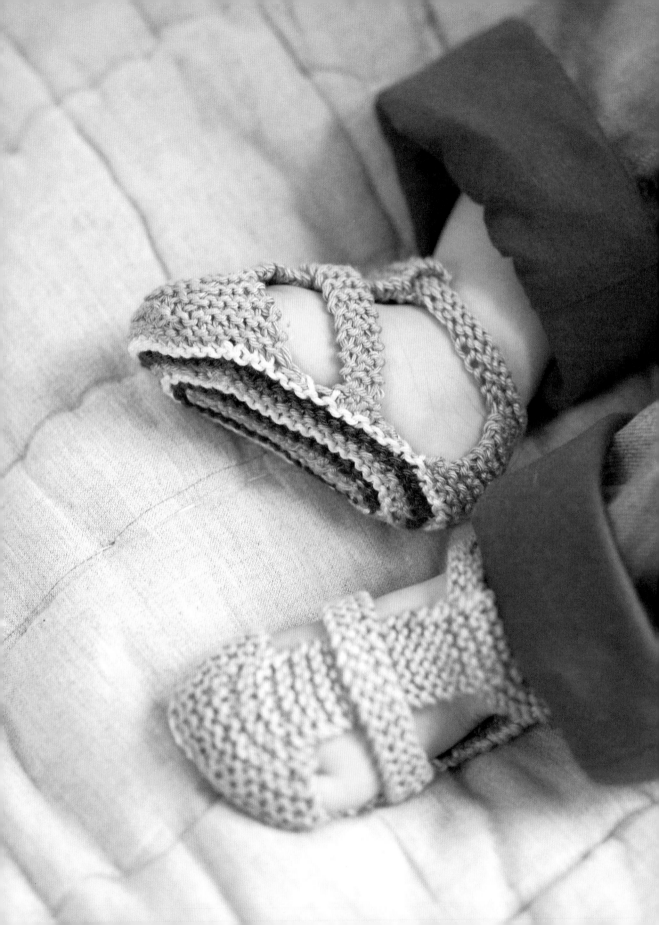

Roman sandals

Feel like a Roman holiday? In no time at all, your baby could be wearing these light, pearl cotton sandals just like a little emperor!

SIZES: 3–6 months (9–12 months)

STITCH USED: Garter stitch (see p. 11)

10 x 10 CM (4 x 4 INCH) TENSION SQUARE IN GARTER STITCH: 24 stitches x 50 rows, using 3 mm (US 2/UK 11) needles

MATERIALS AND TOOLS

1 ball of pearl cotton yarn in Silver Grey
1 ball of pearl cotton yarn in Navy
1 ball of pearl cotton yarn in Sky (or Pink)
One pair of 3 mm (US 2/UK 11) needles
1 wool needle
2 small press-studs
2 decorative buttons
2 safety pins

INSTRUCTIONS

The instructions for the Pink version are given in *italics*, in parentheses after the Silver Grey version. When only one colour is given, it applies to both versions.

Begin at the sole

Cast on 32 (36) stitches in Silver Grey (*Pink*). Change to Navy.

Row 1: Knit.

Row 2: Knit 1, make 1, knit 14 (16), make 1, knit 2, make 1, knit 14 (16), make 1, knit 1. Change to Sky (*Silver Grey*).

Row 3: Knit.

Row 4: Knit 2, make 1, knit 14 (16), make 1, knit 4, make 1, knit 14 (16), make 1, knit 2. Change to Silver Grey (*Pink*).

Row 5: Knit.

Row 6: Knit 3, make 1, knit 14 (16), make 1, knit 6, make 1, knit 14 (16), make 1, knit 3. Change to Navy.

Row 7: Knit.

Row 8: Knit 4, make 1, knit 14 (16), make 1, knit 8, make 1, knit 14 (16), make 1, knit 4. Change to Sky (*Silver Grey*).

Row 9: Knit.

Row 10: Knit 5, make 1, knit 14 (16), make 1, knit 10, make 1, knit 14 (16), make 1, knit 5 = 52 (56) stitches.

Cut the Sky and Navy (*Navy and Silver Grey*) yarn, leaving a length of a few centimetres, then darn them in with the wool needle.

Shape toe and instep

Continuing with the Silver Grey (*Pink*) yarn, knit 8 (9), cast off 2 stitches, knit 4, cast off 2 stitches, knit 20 (22), cast off 2 stitches, knit 4, cast off 2 stitches, knit 8 (9). Cut the yarn, leaving a length of a few centimetres and transfer the last 8 (9) stitches and the next 4 onto a safety pin.

Continuing in Silver Grey (*Pink*), join in the yarn and knit the 20 (22) centre stitches, then transfer the next 4 stitches and the 8 (9) last stitches onto another safety pin.

Knit a further 2 rows on the centre 20 (22) stitches.

Shape wide centre strap

Next row: Knit 6 (7), knit 2 together, knit 4, knit 2 together, knit 6 (7).

Next and every alternate row: Knit.

Next row: Knit 5 (6), knit 2 together, knit 4, knit 2 together, knit 5 (6).

Next row: Knit 4 (5), knit 2 together, knit 4, knit 2 together, knit 4 (5).

Next row: Knit 3 (4), knit 2 together, knit 4, knit 2 together, knit 3 (4) = 12 (14) stitches.

(For the 9–12 months size only:

Next row: Knit 3, knit 2 together, knit 4, knit 2 together, knit 3 = 12 stitches.)

Both sizes. Next row: Knit 1, knit 2 together (5 times), knit 1.

Continue on these 7 stitches for 7 (8) cm, then cast off all remaining stitches.

Shape thin instep strap

Pick up 4 stitches left on hold on one of the safety pins and work in garter stitch using the Silver Grey (*Pink*) yarn for 8.5 (9) cm (3¼/ 3½ inch), then cast off.

Shape heel and ankle strap

Pick up the 8 (9) + 8 (9) stitches on hold on the safety pins. Still using the Silver Grey (*Pink*) yarn, knit 7 (8), knit 2 together, knit 7 (8) = 15 (17) stitches. Continue straight in garter stitch for 14 (17) rows, then, at the beginning of the 15th (18th) row, cast on 22 (24) stitches for the strap, making 37 (41) stitches in total. Knit 3 (4) rows and cast off all remaining stitches.

TO MAKE UP

Fold the bootie with right sides together and stitch the seam to close up the sole and heel. Darn in any loose ends. Fold over 1 cm (½ inch) at the end of the centre strap and catch in place to form a casing for the ankle strap, then thread the strap through. Sew on both parts of the press-stud to secure the strap to the bootie, then sew a decorative button on top. Sew the 4-stitch instep strap to the 4 stitches left on hold on the other side of the sole.

Important: Make sure you make the strap of the second bootie a mirror-image of the first.

Magic moccasins

Here are six customised little slip-on shoes based on the same knitting pattern —
for six completely different styles.

Basic moccasins

SIZES: 3–6 months (9–12 months)

STITCHES USED: Stocking stitch (see p. 11) and garter
stitch (see p. 11)

**10 x 10 CM (4 x 4 INCH) TENSION SQUARE IN
STOCKING STITCH**: 25 stitches x 40 rows, using 3 mm
(US 2/UK 11) needles

MATERIALS AND TOOLS
1 ball of alpaca yarn
One pair of 3 mm (US 2/UK 11) needles
1 wool needle

INSTRUCTIONS

Begin at the sole

Cast on 20 (24) stitches and work in garter stitch.

Row 1 and all odd rows: Knit.

Rows 2, 4, 6, 8 (and Row 10 for the 9–12 months size):
Knit 1, make 1 (see p. 13), knit to the last stitch, make 1,
knit 1 = 28 (34) stitches.

Work 3 (5) more rows in garter stitch.

Rows 12 (16), 14 (18), 16 (20), 18 (22 and 24):
Knit 2 together, knit to the last 2 stitches, knit 2 together.

Row 19 (25): Knit.

For the bootie upper

Row 1: Cast on 7 (9) stitches at the beginning of the row and
knit to the end of the row = 27 (33) stitches.

Row 2: Purl 1, make 1, purl to the end of the row.

Row 3: Knit.

Repeat these last 2 rows 2 (3) more times = 30 (37) stitches.

Row 8 (10): Purl 1, make 1, purl 12 (17), knit 17 (19).

Row 9 (11): Knit.

Row 10 (12): Purl 1, make 1, purl 13 (18), knit 17 (19).

Row 11 (13): Cast off 15 (17) stitches, knit to the end of the
row = 17 (22) stitches.

Row 12 (14): Purl 15 (20), knit 2.

Row 13 (15): Knit.

Rows 14 to 23 (15 to 25): Repeat the last 2 rows 5 more
times.

Row 24 (26): Purl 15 (20), knit 2.

Row 25 (27): Cast on 15 (17) stitches at the beginning of the
row and knit to the end of the row = 32 (39) stitches.

Row 26 (28): Purl 2 together, purl 13 (18), knit 17 (19).

Row 27 (29): Knit.

Row 28 (30): Purl 2 together, purl 12 (17), knit 17 (19).

Rows 29 to 34 (31 to 36): Work in stocking stitch, purling
2 together at the beginning of each purl row.

Cast off all remaining stitches.

TO MAKE UP

With right sides together, sew up the heel seam. Pin the
upper to the sole, easing the upper to fit around the toe area,
and sew them together. Darn in the ends. Make a second
moccasin in the same way.

A

B

Duplicate stitch (Swiss darning)

• Take a length of yarn in a contrasting colour. Bringing
the needle from the back of the work, push it to the
front at the point of a 'V' stitch. Pull the yarn through,
taking care to leave about 10 cm (4 inches) at the back,
to be sewn in later, on the wrong side of the work.

• Slide the needle from right to left behind the stocking
stitch directly above, and bring the needle back out,
pulling gently on the yarn.

• Insert the needle again at the base of the first V,
pushing it through, this time from front to back.
Pull gently.

Easy variations

Little hearts

MATERIALS AND TOOLS

2 hearts in light iron-on felt

Using a hot iron, apply a heart to the top of the foot of each bootie, being careful not to heat the booties for too long. Make sure the heart is attached firmly. To be safe, use a couple of stitches to securely fasten the heart.

Flower buds

MATERIALS AND TOOLS

26 small fabric flowers in different shades of blue
26 seed beads
Reel of linen thread (strong thread)
1 sewing needle

To sew on a flower, push the needle up through the bootie and the flower, thread on a bead to represent the centre of the flower, then push the needle back through the flower and the bootie. Make a very strong knot on the wrong side so that the beads can't be pulled off.
Important: These booties should be gently hand-washed.

Velvet edging

MATERIALS AND TOOLS

40 cm (16 inch) velvet braid
1 reel of thread
1 sewing needle

Run a line of gathering thread along one edge of 20 cm (8 inch) of braid. Pin it around the ankle of the bootie, then pull it up to fit and sew it on securely. Repeat for the second bootie.

Passementerie flower

MATERIALS AND TOOLS

2 small cotton crochet flowers
1 reel of thread
1 sewing needle

Position each flower on top of a bootie using a pin, then sew on securely using small, tight stitches.

Tassels

MATERIALS AND TOOLS

2 small braid tassels
1 wool needle

Pass the two ends of each of the tassel cords through the bootie, spaced by 1 stitch. Knot them together very firmly on the inside of the bootie.

Jacquard flowers

MATERIALS AND TOOLS

Some knitting yarn in a contrasting colour
1 wool needle

On the upper of each bootie, embroider the motif in duplicate stitch (see opposite), following the jacquard chart.

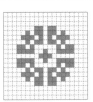

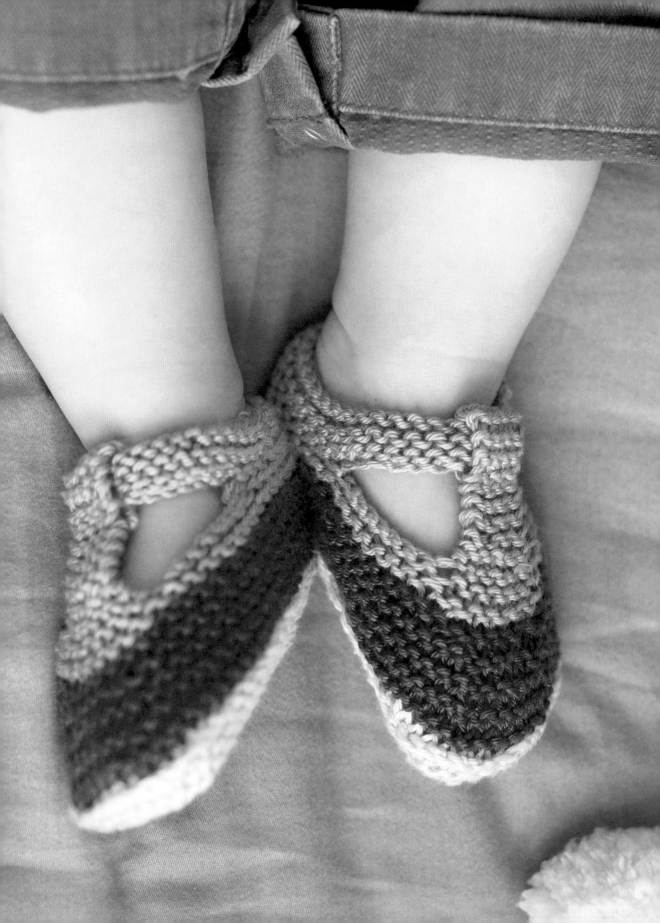

Summer at the beach

In summer, babies like to show off their little feet, but also their pretty sandals!

SIZES: 3–6 months (9–12 months)

STITCH USED: Garter stitch (see p. 11)

10 x 10 CM (4 x 4 INCH) TENSION SQUARE IN GARTER STITCH: 24 stitches x 50 rows, using 3 mm (US 2/UK 11) needles

MATERIALS AND TOOLS

1 ball of pearl cotton yarn in Sky
1 ball of pearl cotton yarn in Navy
1 ball of pearl cotton yarn in Silver Grey
One pair of 3 mm (US 2/UK 11) needles
1 wool needle
2 small press-studs
2 small decorative buttons
2 safety pins

INSTRUCTIONS

For the sole

Begin the bootie at the centre of the sole. Cast on 32 (36) stitches in Sky and knit 1 row.

Row 2: Knit 1, make 1, knit 14 (16), make 1, knit 2, make 1, knit 14 (16), make 1, knit 1 = 36 (40) stitches.

Row 3 and every alternate row: Knit.

Row 4: Knit 2, make 1, knit 14 (16), make 1, knit 4, make 1, knit 14 (16), make 1, knit 2.

Row 6: Knit 3, make 1, knit 14 (16), make 1, knit 6, make 1, knit 14 (16), make 1, knit 3.

Row 8: Knit 4, make 1, knit 14 (16), make 1, knit 8, make 1, knit 14 (16), make 1, knit 4.

Row 10: Knit 5, make 1, knit 14 (16), make 1, knit 10, make 1, knit 14 (16), make 1, knit 5 = 52 (56) stitches.

For the bootie upper

Change to Navy. Knit 2 rows without shaping.

Next row: Knit 22 (24), knit 2 together, knit 4, knit 2 together, knit 22 (24) = 50 (54) stitches.

Next and every alternate row: Knit.

Next row: Knit 21 (23), knit 2 together, knit 4, knit 2 together, knit 21 (23) = 48 (52) stitches.

Continue in this manner, decreasing 1 stitch on either side of the centre 4 stitches in every 2nd row until 44 (46) stitches remain.

Change to Pearl Grey yarn and knit 3 rows without shaping.

Next row: Knit 10 (11), cast off 7 stitches, knit 8, cast off 9 stitches, and knit the remaining 10 (11) stitches.

Next row: Place the first 10 (11) stitches on hold on a safety pin. Knit the centre 8 stitches (centre strap) and place the last 10 (11) stitches on a second safety pin.

Shape centre strap as follows: Knit 2 (4) rows on the 8 stitches of the centre strap.

Row 3 (5): Knit 1, knit 2 together, knit 2, knit 2 together, knit 1.

Row 4 (6): Knit.

Row 5 (7): Knit 2, knit 2 together, knit 2.

Continue on these 5 remaining stitches without shaping and cast off in the 28th (30th) row.

TO MAKE UP

Fold the bootie and stitch the sole and heel seams. Using a knitting needle and Silver Grey yarn, pick up the 20 (22) stitches on hold on the safety pins. Cast on 18 (20) stitches at one end for the ankle strap. Knit 5 rows, then cast off. Darn in any ends. Fold over 1 cm (½ inch) at the end of the centre strap and catch in place to form a casing, then thread the ankle strap through the casing. Sew on both parts of the press-stud to secure the strap to the bootie and sew a decorative button on top. If you like, embroider a row of herringbone stitch on the last Sky row of the sole.

Important: Make sure you make the strap of the second bootie a mirror-image of the first.

Super simple

These booties are very simple to make: you basically just knit a strip in garter stitch. Cleverly sewn together, this pattern makes adorable booties.

SIZES: 3–6 months (9–12 months)

STITCH USED: Garter stitch (see p. 11)

10 x 10 CM (4 x 4 INCH) TENSION SQUARE IN GARTER STITCH: 22 stitches x 20 rows, using 3.5 mm (US 4/UK 10) needles

MATERIALS AND TOOLS
1 ball of bamboo yarn in Pearl
One pair of 3.5 mm (US 4/UK 10) knitting needles
4 small shank-style knotted buttons
1 wool needle

INSTRUCTIONS

Cast on 27 (29) stitches and work 9 (11) cm (3½/ 4¼ inch) in garter stitch.

Next 3 rows: Knit 2 together, 2 by 2, until you have 4 stitches left.

TO MAKE UP

Cut the yarn, leaving a good length of tail, thread the yarn onto the wool needle, pass it through the 4 remaining stitches, pull up tightly and fasten off to create the toe end of the bootie.

Fold the other end of the strip in half lengthwise, right sides facing each other, and sew the short edges together to form the back of the heel. Stitching from the toe end, sew the edges together along the top for about one third of the length of the foot, forming the instep seam.

Sew on two small buttons to decorate the instep of the bootie.

Make the second bootie in the same way.

Irish Miss

A little Irish folklore is worked into these traditional cabled booties.
Cable stitch sometimes seems a little tricky for beginners, but just practise making a sample
before you start and you'll soon be able to tackle it without any problems.

SIZES: 3–6 months (9–12 months)

STITCHES USED: Garter stitch (see p. 11) and cable stitch (see below)

10 x 10 CM (4 x 4 INCH) TENSION SQUARE IN GARTER STITCH: 25 stitches x 52 rows, using 2.75 mm (US 2/UK 12) needles

MATERIALS AND TOOLS
1 ball of alpaca yarn in Pearl Grey
1 ball of alpaca yarn in Purple
One pair of 2.75 mm (US 2/UK 12) needles
One cable needle
1 wool needle

Cable stitch motif

This motif is worked over 8 rows. (Instructions for the 9–12 months size are given in parentheses.)

Row 1: *Purl 1, knit 4**, repeat from * to ** to the last 2 (1) stitch/es, purl 2 (1).

Row 2: Knit 1 (0), *knit 1, purl 4**, repeat from * to ** to the last stitch, knit 1.

Row 3: *Purl 2, knit 2, purl 2, 1 left-twisting 4-stitch cable (see page 14)**, repeat from * to ** to the last 2 (6) stitches, purl 2 (purl 2, knit 2, purl 2).

Row 4: Knit 2 (knit 2, purl 2, knit 2), *purl 4, knit 2, purl 2, knit 2**, repeat from * to ** to the end of the row.

Row 5: Work as for Row 1.

Row 6: Work as for Row 2.

Row 7: *Purl 2, knit 2, purl 2, knit 4**, repeat from * to ** to last 2 (6) stitches, purl 2 (purl 2, knit 2, purl 2).

Row 8: Knit 2 (knit 2, purl 2, knit 2), *purl 4, knit 2, purl 2, knit 2**, repeat from * to ** to the end of the row.

INSTRUCTIONS

Begin at the ankle

Cast on 42 (46) stitches in Pearl Grey. Work 4 cable stitch motifs (as above), minus the last row in the last motif = 31 rows.

Row 32: Purl, decreasing 1 stitch 6 times evenly across the row = 36 (40) stitches.

Cut the Pearl Grey yarn and begin the instep of the bootie using the Purple yarn, in garter stitch.

Shape the instep

Knit 24 (27), turn the work, knit 12 (14), turn the work.

Continue on these 12 (14) centre stitches (leaving 12 (13) stitches on the needle at each end) and work 23 (27) rows of garter stitch.

Shape the sides

Next row: Knit the centre 12 (14) stitches, then pick up and knit 12 (14) stitches along the edge of the instep, then pick back up and knit the next 12 (13) stitches that have been on hold.

Next row: Knit 36 (41), then pick up and knit 12 (14) stitches along the other edge of the instep, then knit the 12 (13) remaining stitches on hold = 60 (68) stitches.

Work 16 (18) rows in garter stitch.

Shape the sole

Next row: Knit 1, knit 2 together, knit 25 (29), knit 2 together (twice), knit 25 (29), knit 2 together, knit 1.

Next row: Knit.

Next row: Knit 1, knit 2 together, knit 23 (27), knit 2 together (twice), knit 23 (27), knit 2 together, knit 1.

Next row: Knit.

Next row: Knit 1, knit 2 together, knit 21 (25), knit 2 together (twice), knit 21 (25), knit 2 together, knit 1.

Next row: Knit.

Cast off loosely.

TO MAKE UP

Sew up the centre back and sole seams of the sock and sew in any loose ends. Make the second sock in the same way.

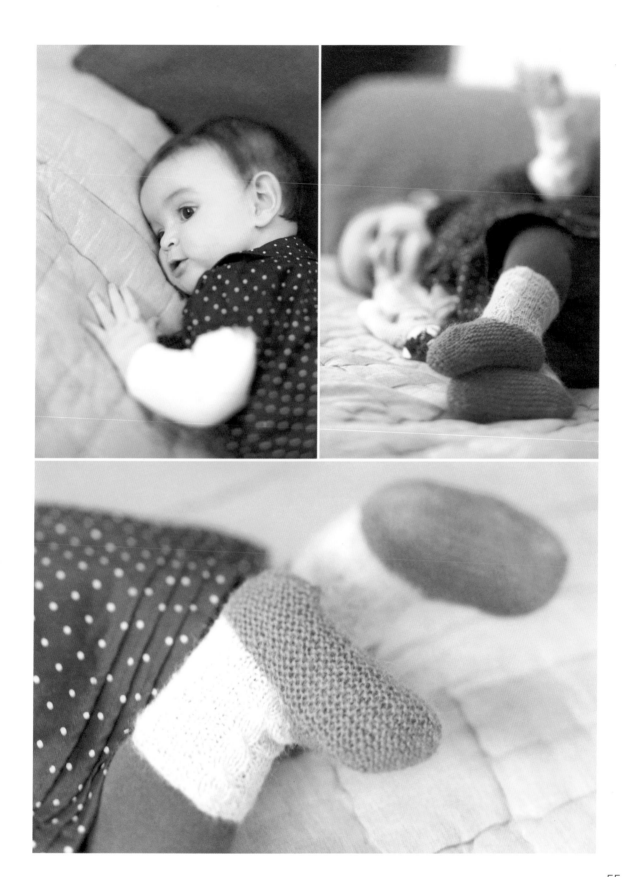

Cables and stripes

These cheerful booties feature the same cable pattern as the booties on page 54, but are given a jaunty look with the addition of stripes.

SIZES: 3–6 months (9–12 months)

STITCHES USED: Garter stitch (see p. 11) and cable stitch (see p. 54)

10 x 10 CM (4 x 4 INCH) TENSION SQUARE IN GARTER STITCH: 25 stitches x 52 rows, using 2.75 mm (US 2/UK 12) needles

MATERIALS AND TOOLS
1 ball of alpaca yarn in Grey
1 ball of alpaca yarn in Plum
One pair of 2.75 mm (US 2/UK 12) needles
One cable needle
1 wool needle

INSTRUCTIONS

Begin at the ankle

Cast on 42 (46) stitches in Grey. Work 4 cable stitch motifs (as above), minus the last row in the last motif = 31 rows.

Row 32: Purl, decreasing 1 stitch 6 times evenly across the row = 36 (40) stitches.

Cut the Grey yarn and begin the instep of the bootie using the Plum yarn. Note that the whole foot is worked in striped garter stitch: 2 rows Plum, 2 rows Grey.

Shape the instep

Knit 24 (27), turn the work, knit 12 (14), turn the work.

Continue on these 12 (14) centre stitches (leaving 12 (13) stitches on the needle at each end) and work 23 (27) rows of garter stitch, keeping the stripes correct.

Shape the sides

Next row: Knit the centre 12 (14) stitches, then pick up and knit 12 (14) stitches along the edge of the instep, then pick back up and knit the next 12 (13) stitches that have been on hold.

Next row: Knit 36 (41), then pick up and knit 12 (14) stitches along the other edge of the instep, then knit the 12 (13) remaining stitches on hold = 60 (68) stitches.

Work 16 (18) rows in garter stitch, keeping stripes correct.

Shape the sole

Next row: Knit 1, knit 2 together, knit 25 (29), knit 2 together (twice), knit 25 (29), knit 2 together, knit 1.

Next row: Knit.

Next row: Knit 1, knit 2 together, knit 23 (27), knit 2 together (twice), knit 23 (27), knit 2 together, knit 1.

Next row: Knit.

Next row: Knit 1, knit 2 together, knit 21 (25), knit 2 together (twice), knit 21 (25), knit 2 together, knit 1.

Next row: Knit.

Cast off loosely.

TO MAKE UP

Sew up the centre back and sole seams of the sock and sew in any loose ends. Make the second sock in the same way.

Playful stripes

Nothing like brightly coloured beanies and booties to add colour to the cold of winter.

Striped beanie

Sizes: 3–6 months (9–12 months)

Stitch used: Garter stitch (see p. 11)

10 x 10 cm (4 x 4 inch) tension square in garter stitch: 26 stitches x 55 rows, using 3 mm (US 2/UK 11) needles

Materials and tools
1 ball of pure wool in Plum (A)
1 ball of pure wool in Fuchsia (B)
1 ball of pure wool in Candy Pink (C)
One pair of 3 mm (US 2/UK 11) needles
1 wool needle

Instructions

Cast on 86 (98) stitches in yarn colour B. Change to yarn A, and and work in garter stitch as follows:

Work 2 rows in yarn A, 2 rows in yarn C, 2 rows in yarn A, 2 rows in yarn B, and so on for 11 (14) cm (4¼/ 5½ inches).

Next row: Knit 1, *knit 2 together, knit 10**, repeat from * to ** until the last stitch, knit 1.

Next row: Knit.

Next row: Knit 1, *knit 2 together, knit 9**, repeat from * to ** until the last stitch, knit 1.

Next row: Knit.

Next row: Knit 1, *knit 2 together, knit 8**, repeat from * to ** until the last stitch, knit 1.

Next row: Knit.

Next row: Knit 1, *knit 2 together, knit 7**, repeat from * to ** until the last stitch, knit 1.

Next row: Knit.

Next row: Knit 1, *knit 2 together, knit 6**, repeat from * to ** until the last stitch, knit 1.

Next row: Knit.

Next row: Knit 1, *knit 2 together, knit 5**, repeat from * to ** until the last stitch, knit 1.

Next row: Knit.

Next row: Knit 1, *knit 2 together, knit 4**, repeat from * to ** until the last stitch, knit 1.

Next row: Knit.

Next row: Knit 1, *knit 2 together, knit 3**, repeat from * to ** until the last stitch, knit 1.

Next row: Knit.

Next row: Knit 1, *knit 2 together, knit 2**, repeat from * to ** until the last stitch, knit 1.

Next row: Knit.

Next row: Knit 1, *knit 2 together, knit 1**, repeat from * to ** until the last stitch, knit 1.

Next row: Knit.

Next row: Knit 1, knit 2 together until the last stitch, knit 1.

Cut the yarn, leaving a 30 cm (12 inch) length, thread it onto a wool needle then thread it through the remaining stitches.

To make up

Pull gently on the thread to gather the top of the beanie, then stitch the centre back seam, on the wrong side of the work, working 1 stitch inside the edge.

Change to working on the right side of the work for the last 2 cm (¾ inch) so that the seam is reversed for the cuff section of the beanie. Darn in any loose threads.

continued...

Striped booties

SIZES: 3–6 months (9–12 months)

STITCHES USED: Garter stitch (see p. 11), stocking stitch (see p. 11) and single rib (see p. 12)

10 x 10 CM (4 x 4 INCH) TENSION SQUARE IN GARTER STITCH: 26 stitches x 55 rows, using 3 mm (US 2/UK 11) needles

MATERIALS AND TOOLS:
1 ball of pure wool in Plum (A)
1 ball of pure wool in Fuchsia (B)
One pair of 3 mm (US 2/UK 11) needles
1 wool needle

INSTRUCTIONS

Begin at the ankle

Cast on 42 (44) stitches in yarn colour B. Change to yarn A and work 6 (7) cm (2½/ 2¾ inches) in single rib, working 2 stitches together at the end of the last row.

Work these 41 (43) stitches in stocking stitch for 4 rows.

Shape the instep

Knit 28 (29), turn the work, purl 15 purl, turn.

Continue on these 15 centre stitches (leaving 13 (14) stitches on the needle at each end) and work 22 (24) rows of stocking stitch. Cut the yarn and leave these stitches on the needle.

Shape the sides

Rejoin the yarn to the the first 13 (14) stitches left on hold and knit, then pick up 11 (12) stitches evenly on the selvedge of the instep, then work the 15 centre stitches, pick up 11 (12) stitches on the other instep selvedge, and work the last 13 (14) stitches on hold = 63 (67) stitches.

Next row: Knit, then proceed as follows:

Row 1:Yarn A, knit to end of row.

Rows 2 and 3: Yarn B, knit to end of row.

Rows 4 and 5: Yarn A, knit to end of row.

Repeat rows 2 to 5 twice. Cut off yarn B.

(**For the 9–12 months size**: Work 2 extra rows, in yarn A).

Shape the heel and toe

Next row: Knit 1, knit 2 together, knit 25 (27), knit 2 together, knit 3, knit 2 together, knit 25 (27), knit 2 together, knit 1.

Next row: Knit 26 (28), knit 2 together, knit 3, knit 2 together, knit 26 (28).

Next row: Knit 1, knit 2 together, knit 22 (24), knit 2 together, knit 3, knit 2 together, knit 22 (24), knit 2 together, knit 1.

Next row: Knit 23 (25), knit 2 together, knit 3, knit 2 together, knit 23 (25).

Next row: Knit 1, knit 2 together, knit 19 (21), knit 2 together, knit 3, knit 2 together, knit 19 (21), knit 2 together, knit 1.

Cast off all remaining stitches.

TO MAKE UP

Sew up the foot seam and the centre back seam, 1 stitch inside the edge on the wrong side. Change to sewing on the right side for the last 2 cm (¾ inch) so that the seam is reversed for the turn-over on the cuff. Darn in the loose ends.

Make the second bootie in the same way.